For Gary, Taryn, and Tyler, for whom I don't cook as often as I should.

–A.E.H.

To my wife Karen. Whatever she bakes smells like home.

–B.D.

Pretzels
by the
Dozen

Truth and Inspiration
with a Heart-Shaped Twist

Written By

Angela Elwell Hunt

Illustrated by

Bill Dodge

Zonderkidz

I

piece of soft dough,
rolled long and round.

2

ends of dough rope,
twisted and pressed down.

No one knows the name of the monk who made
the first pretzel in A.D. 610, but we do know he
called his creation pretiolas.

3

open windows
face the rising sun.
Father, Son, and Holy Spirit
are the Three-in-One.

4

hungry children,
praying to the Lord.
When their prayers are said,
they earn a tasty, warm reward.

That first pretzel-making monk gave pretzels to the children as a reward for learning their prayers. The three holes in a pretzel are said to represent the Trinity: one God in three persons.

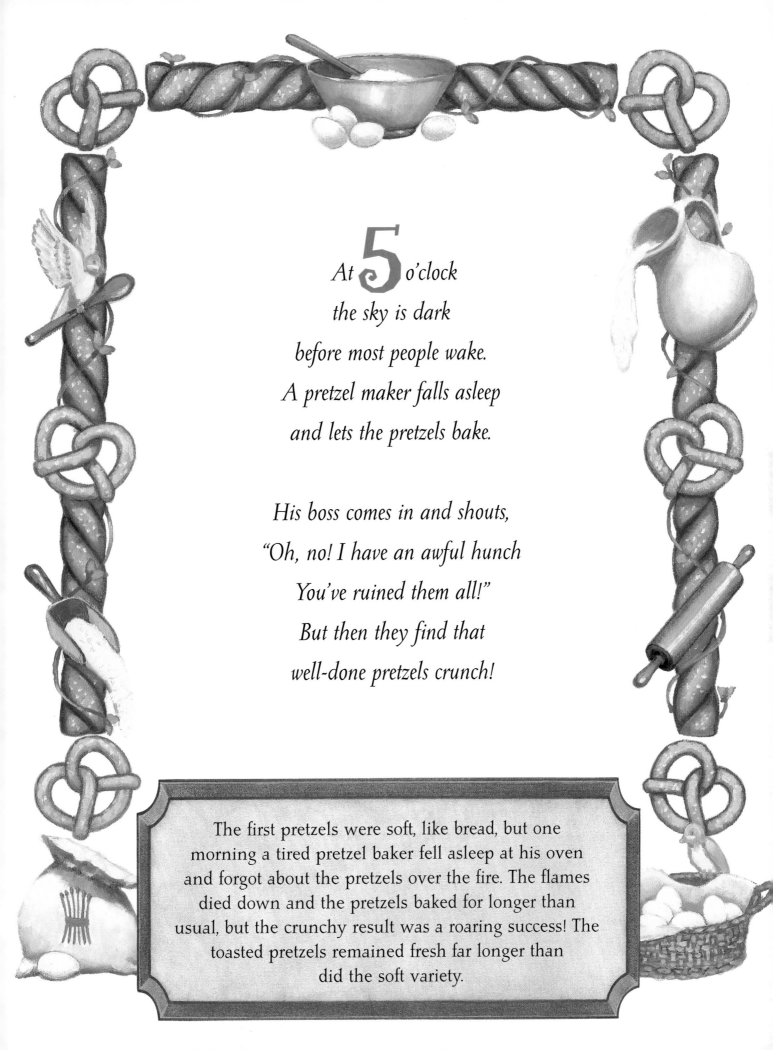

At **5** o'clock
the sky is dark
before most people wake.
A pretzel maker falls asleep
and lets the pretzels bake.

His boss comes in and shouts,
"Oh, no! I have an awful hunch
You've ruined them all!"
But then they find that
well-done pretzels crunch!

The first pretzels were soft, like bread, but one morning a tired pretzel baker fell asleep at his oven and forgot about the pretzels over the fire. The flames died down and the pretzels baked for longer than usual, but the crunchy result was a roaring success! The toasted pretzels remained fresh far longer than did the soft variety.

6

royal hearts are joined today—
parents, bride, and groom,
Happy that the Lord has spread
his love throughout the room.

The bride picks up the wedding bread
and gives her groom a grin.
They say a prayer, they make a wish,
they pull—to see who wins!

A woodcut dating from 1614 pictures a pretzel used as a
marriage knot to unite two royal families. Wishing on a pretzel became
a common ritual at weddings. The bride and groom made a wish and
pulled. Whoever broke off the larger piece of pretzel won, but since the
bride and groom each wished for happiness together,
both were winners!

children on New Year's Day,
believing God is good,
Hang pretzels around their necks
and frolic in the woods.

A pretzel necklace, they believe,
insures God's love and joy,
And so a yummy snack is given
to every girl and boy!

Pretzels began to symbolize long life and God's blessing. On New Year's Day, children of the Black Forest wore pretzels on loops around their necks.

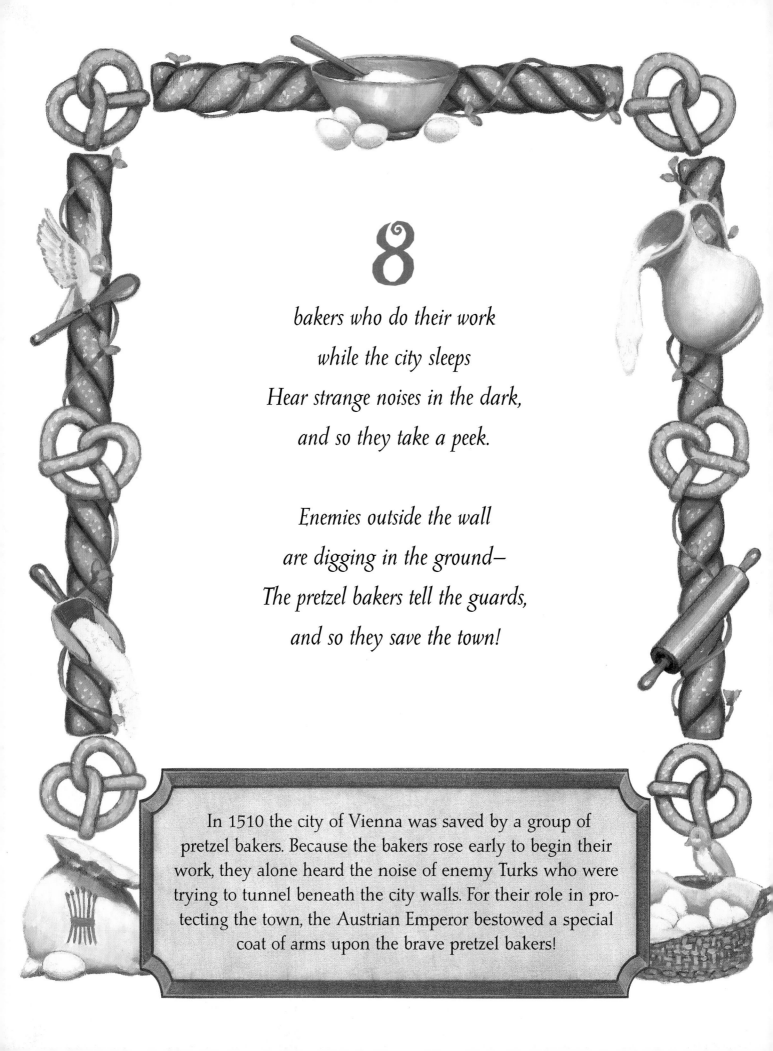

8

bakers who do their work

while the city sleeps

Hear strange noises in the dark,

and so they take a peek.

Enemies outside the wall

are digging in the ground—

The pretzel bakers tell the guards,

and so they save the town!

In 1510 the city of Vienna was saved by a group of pretzel bakers. Because the bakers rose early to begin their work, they alone heard the noise of enemy Turks who were trying to tunnel beneath the city walls. For their role in protecting the town, the Austrian Emperor bestowed a special coat of arms upon the brave pretzel bakers!

9
men are paraded through
a town while neighbors cheer,
Celebrating marriages
of five-and-twenty years.

To show their godly gratitude
and prove they're not regretful,
The men toss candy, fruit, and coins,
along with crispy pretzels.

The people of Sigmaringen, a town in old
Germany, celebrated silver wedding anniver-
saries with pretzel parades!

10

Pilgrims leave the Mayflower,
their hopes and faith in God.
They'll establish homes and towns
upon a foreign sod.

From England they bring books and tools,
faith and lots of spunk,
And recipes for warm pretzels
are packed within their trunks!

Though we don't know for certain that the children on
the Mayflower ate pretzels, we are sure the recipe
arrived with settlers to the New World.

II

natives leave their homes
to visit Jochem Wessels.
They offer beads and pots and furs
to trade for Jochem's pretzels.

Jochem gladly makes the deal,
but his neighbors are most speedy.
For selling pretzels, he goes to jail—
for his neighbors are quite greedy.

Jochem Wessels and his wife really were arrested for selling pretzels to Native Americans in 1652. The greedy colonists did not want to share their favorite food with their new neighbors!

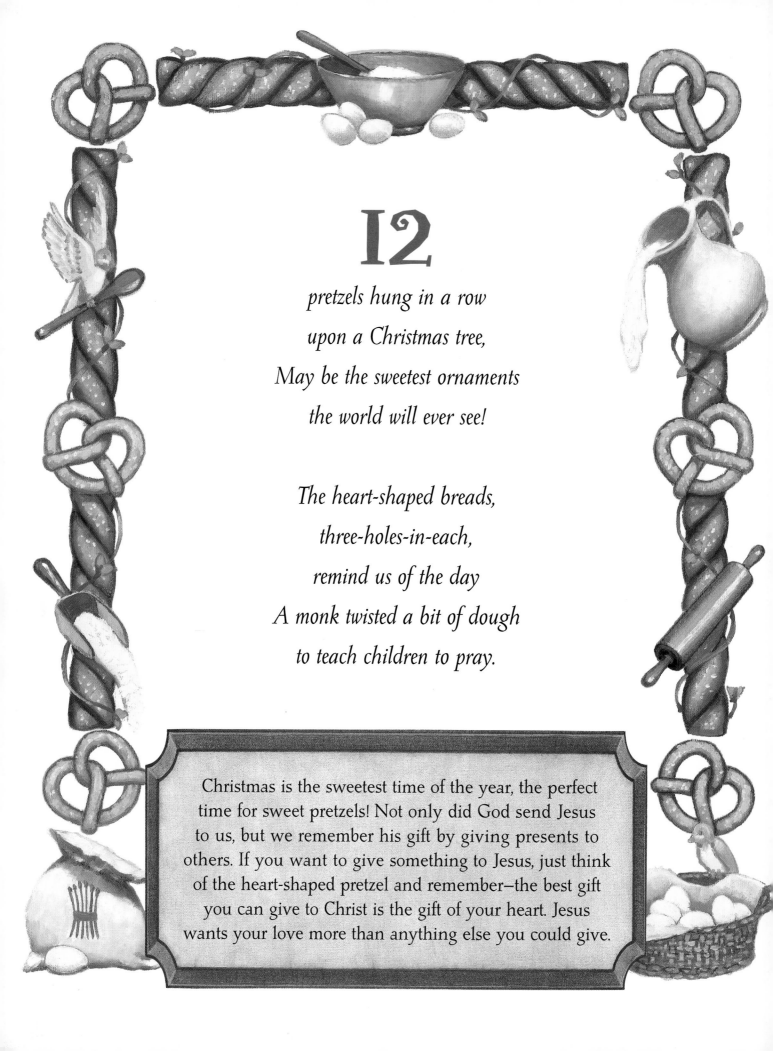

12

pretzels hung in a row
upon a Christmas tree,
May be the sweetest ornaments
the world will ever see!

The heart-shaped breads,
three-holes-in-each,
remind us of the day
A monk twisted a bit of dough
to teach children to pray.

Christmas is the sweetest time of the year, the perfect time for sweet pretzels! Not only did God send Jesus to us, but we remember his gift by giving presents to others. If you want to give something to Jesus, just think of the heart-shaped pretzel and remember—the best gift you can give to Christ is the gift of your heart. Jesus wants your love more than anything else you could give.

On New Year's Eve in bright Times Square
they drop a shining ball.
Millions cheer for the new year
while fireworks spark and fall.

In quiet Lititz, miles away,
celebrations aren't as stressful.
As the clock ticks down, they raise a cheer
and drop a giant pretzel!

In the late 1850s a traveler passing through Lititz, Pennsylvania, exchanged an improved pretzel recipe for a hot meal. The traveler moved on, and the recipe was given to Julius Sturgis, who in 1861 opened America's first commercial pretzel bakery in Lititz. The Julius Sturgis Pretzel House is still making pretzels today!

Bake a Batch of Perfect Pretzels!

You and an adult can bake pretzels together!

You will need:

A cookie sheet sprayed with nonstick spray

1 $\frac{1}{2}$ teaspoon yeast

$\frac{1}{2}$ teaspoon brown sugar

a dash of regular salt

1 $\frac{1}{2}$ cup warm water

4 cups flour

2 cups warm water

2 teaspoons baking soda

1 egg, 1 tablespoon water, and coarse salt
(for salty pretzels) or

$\frac{1}{2}$ cup melted butter, and
white or brown sugar (for sweet pretzels)

1. In a small bowl mix together the 1 $\frac{1}{2}$ teaspoon yeast, $\frac{1}{2}$ teaspoon brown sugar, dash of salt, and 1 $\frac{1}{2}$ cup warm water. Stir with a wooden spoon, and set aside for about five minutes.

2. In a large bowl measure out 4 cups of flour.

3. After five minutes, when the yeast mixture is a little bubbly, pour it into the large bowl with the flour. Stir everything together with a wooden spoon, and finish the mixing with your clean hands! When the dough is smooth, cover with a clean kitchen towel and let the dough rest for about an hour.

4. After an hour, preheat the oven to 550 degrees. This is very hot, so make sure an adult is around to help!

5. In another small bowl pour 2 cups of warm water and add the 2 teaspoons of baking soda. This is the "soda water."

6. Pull off a piece of dough about the size of a golf ball. Squeeze it in your hands until there are no dry bits. When the entire piece is smooth, place it on a clean countertop and roll it into the shape of a snake. (If the dough sticks, sprinkle a little flour on the countertop.)

7. Once the dough is rolled out into a long, thin snake, pick up the two ends, twist them, and press them into the upper loop of the circle. Don't worry if your pretzel isn't perfect.

8. Dip your entire pretzel into the soda water and then set it on the cookie sheet that has been sprayed with nonstick spray. Continue until the cookie sheet is filled.

9. If you want to make salty pretzels, in another small bowl, beat together the egg and one tablespoon of water. Now brush your pretzels with the egg mixture, and then sprinkle with the coarse salt. (If you want to make sweet pretzels, ignore this step.)

10. Have an adult place the cookie sheet in the hot oven, and bake at 550 degrees for eight minutes, or until pretzels are beginning to turn golden brown. Have the adult remove the cookie sheet from the oven.

11. If you want to make sweet pretzels, while they are still on the cookie sheet and hot, brush the pretzels with melted butter and then sprinkle with white or brown sugar.

Pretzels by the Dozen

Copyright © 2002 by Angela Elwell Hunt
Illustrations copyright © 2002 by Bill Dodge
Requests for information should be addressed to:

Zonderkidz™

The children's group of Zondervan

Grand Rapids, Michigan 49530
www.zonderkidz.com

Zonderkidz is a trademark of Zondervan.

ISBN: 0-310-70173-2

Editing by Gwen Ellis
Art direction and Design by Lisa Workman

Printed in Hong Kong
02 03 04 05/HK/5 4 3 2 1